GW01045205

OUR DAILY FOOD

✠

OUR DAILY FOOD

or

Portions for the Lord's Household

Compiled by

JAMES SMITH

with an Introduction by

JEREMY WALKER

THE BANNER OF TRUTH TRUST

THE BANNER OF TRUTH TRUST

Head Office
3 Murrayfield Road
Edinburgh, EH12 6EL
UK

North America Office
610 Alexander Spring Road
Carlisle, PA 17015
USA

banneroftruth.org

*

ISBN
Print: 978 1 80040 377 2
Epub: 978 1 80040 378 9

*

Typeset in 10.5/13.5 pt Adobe Caslon Pro
at The Banner of Truth Trust, Edinburgh

Printed in the USA by
Versa Press, Inc.,
East Peoria, IL

Introduction

James Smith of Cheltenham is perhaps not a name you know. If you have seen it before, it may have been in a few particular places. You may have noticed a collection of devotions called *The Believer's Daily Remembrancer*, one of the few productions of his pen still more or less available. You may have noted his name as one of the preachers on the occasion of the opening of the Metropolitan Tabernacle in 1861, when he preached a sweet sermon on effectual calling.

Smith had actually served as pastor at the New Park Street Chapel from 1841–1850, preceding the call of Spurgeon in 1854. His first and last pastorates were at Cheltenham, Gloucester. He was, though, a Londoner by birth, having been born in Brentford on 19 November 1802. He was converted in 1819, when he heard a plain man preach an earnest sermon on Mark 8:36, 37: 'For what will it profit a man if he gains the whole world, and loses his own soul? Or what will a man give in exchange for his soul?' Smith was gripped by the preaching, convinced 'that the world, if I could gain it, would be no compensation for the loss of my immortal soul.' Deeply convicted, he cried out to the Lord who granted him peace. He was baptised on 31 March 1820.

As well as serving in a number of churches, James Smith was a prolific writer, and his daily readings and devotionals in particular were highly esteemed and hugely popular. 'My object,' said our author, 'is to lead the mind from self—to Jesus; from sin—to salvation; from the troubles of life—to the comforts of the gospel. My aim is to humble the sinner—and exalt the Saviour; to strip the creature—and place the crown on the head of God's free grace! I cannot ascribe too much to Jesus—or too little to man!'

The devotional text which follows achieves this aim. You will not use this volume to find weighty exegesis of a text. Indeed, one of the challenges we might first face is that the words come to us seemingly robbed of their context. Smith typically isolates not just a verse but even a phrase from that verse, and sets it out and apart in itself. The initial effect may be to create an almost atomistic sense—an apple of gold without a setting of silver, if you will. And yet, as you use the book, you begin to understand what Smith is doing.

While Smith may be assuming a measure of biblical knowledge, his intention seems to be that you should simply dwell upon the atom for a few moments. Look at the idea of the phrase. He wants you to consider its bald, bold truth, starkly alone but not really isolated. That he understands it in its context is typically made clear by the lines of verse which adorn the words of God. They are chosen from any number of sources, some of them perhaps vaguely familiar to those of us who love old hymns as well as new; others appear fresh to us perhaps because they have been rescued from obscurity. Each one sheds light upon the text and gives an insight—perhaps less than an explanation, but certainly more than a hint—of the leading thought that Smith would have us carry away. The net effect is to oblige us to meditate on the truth, to force us to feel the weight of the truth rather than to count the number of the words. He typically captures the core idea of the text, and the verse allows us to consider that idea in a forceful and memorable way.

Some daily devotionals are longer, and demand a fair amount of time. Some are briefer, and take a few moments to read over. These golden nuggets of truth will take only a moment to consider, but will give you matter for a day's consideration and comfort.

JEREMY WALKER

January

1. Lord, let it alone this year also.

—LUKE 13:8.

Lord, melt our hearts to mourn the past,
　And let us henceforth faithful be;
And if this year should be our last,
　Oh may our souls repose with thee.

———

2. Search me, O God, and know my heart: try me, and know my thoughts.

—PSA. 139:23.

Search, O Lord, and cleanse, and save us;
　Heal us by thy power divine;
Burst the bonds that here enslave us,
　That we may be wholly thine.

January

3. The Lord of peace himself give you peace always by all means.

—2 THESS. 3:16.

By thy passion on the tree,
  Let my griefs and troubles cease;
Oh, remember Calvary,
  And give me holy peace.

---

4. Having boldness to enter into the holiest by the blood of Jesus, let us draw near.—HEB. 10:19, 22.

Since by a new and living way
  Access to God is given,
Poor sinners may with boldness pray,
  And earth converse with heaven.

January

5. Remember me, O my God, for good.—NEH. 13:31.

Yes, when these failing lips grow dumb,
  And thought and memory flee;
When thou shalt in thy kingdom come,
  Jesus, remember me.

———————

6. And I will pray the Father, and he shall give you another Comforter, that he may abide with you for ever.

—JOHN 14:16.

Come, Holy Ghost, into my mind,
  Fill me with heavenly light,
Kindle my heart with fervent zeal
  To serve God day and night.

7. It pleased God to reveal his Son in me.—GAL. 1:15, 16.

Father, in me thy Son reveal;
  Teach me to know and do thy will;
Thy saving power and love display,
  And guide me to the realms of day.

---

8. He that loveth me shall be loved of my Father, and I will love him, and will manifest myself to him.—JOHN 14:21.

Lord, send thy blessing from above,
  And sweetly to my soul appear;
Behold me with a Father's love,
  And fill my heart with filial fear.

January

9. The steps of a good man are ordered by the LORD.—PSA. 37:23.

> While passing through the wilderness,
>   Full of temptations and distress,
> What comfort does the thought afford,
>   Our steps are ordered by the Lord!

---

10. We are saved by hope: but hope that is seen is not hope: for what a man seeth, why doth he yet hope for?—ROM. 8:24.

> 'Tis by hope the saints are saved;
>   Living hope to Jesus goes;
> Draws all life through Jesus' merit,
>   And no other Saviour knows.

11. Who are kept by the power of God through faith unto salvation.—1 PET. 1:5.

All who possess true faith and love
　This daily, by experience, prove,
That they who simply put their trust
　In Jesus Christ can ne'er be lost.

---

12. There I will meet with thee, and I will commune with thee from above the mercy seat.—EXOD. 25:22.

From every stormy wind that blows,
　From every swelling tide of woes,
There is a calm, a sure retreat—
　'Tis found beneath the mercy-seat.

January

13. In whom we have redemption through his blood, even the forgiveness of sins.—Col. 1:14.

> Jesus the sacrifice became,
>   To rescue guilty souls from hell;
> The spotless, bleeding, dying Lamb
>   Beneath avenging justice fell.

---

14. A merciful and faithful high priest in things pertaining to God.—Heb. 2:17.

> Clothed with our nature still, he knows
>   The weakness of our frame,
> And how to shield us from the foes
>   Which he himself o'ercame.

15. Blessed are ye that hunger now: for ye shall be filled.—LUKE 6:21.

From him the poor are never driven,
  He lifts the prostrate from the dust;
By him the rebel is forgiven,
  And in his name is taught to trust.

---

16. Unto you therefore which believe he is precious.—I PET. 2:7.

The name of Jesus precious is,
  A rock, a sure defence, a tower;
No name a virtue has like his—
  'Tis life and health, 'tis grace and power.

17. The LORD thy God, he it is that doth go with thee; he will not fail thee, nor forsake thee.—DEUT. 31:6.

> Jesus, when I have safely passed
>   Through every conflict but the last,
> Still, still unchanging, watch beside
>   My painful bed, for thou hast died.

18. It is not in man that walketh to direct his steps.—JER. 10:23.

> The Lord, our leader, goes before—
>   Sufficient he, and none beside;
> And were the dangers many more,
>   We need not fear with such a guide.

January

19. For it is God which worketh in you both to will and to do of his good pleasure.—PHIL. 2:13.

Assisted by his grace,
  We still pursue our way;
And hope at last to reach the prize,
  Secure in endless day.

---

20. Whosoever is born of God doth not commit sin.—I JOHN 3:9.

Teach me by sweet experience, Lord,
  This heavenly birth to know;
And thy perpetual aid afford,
  That I in grace may grow.

January

21. The Spirit of truth, which proceedeth from the Father, he shall testify of me.

—John 15:26.

Come, heavenly Comforter, come!
  Sweet witness of mercy divine,
And make me thy permanent home,
  And seal me eternally thine!

---

22. For to me to live is Christ, and to die is gain.—Phil. 1:21.

Ah, give me, Lord, the single eye
  Which aims at nought but thee;
I fain would live, and yet not I—
  Let Jesus live in me.

23. I will look to the LORD; I will wait for the God of my salvation.

—MIC. 7:7.

None can be so o'erwhelmed with grief,
  But he in Christ may find relief;
All misery, however great,
  His comforts can alleviate.

————

24. Christ died for our sins according to the scriptures.—1 COR. 15:3.

He sunk beneath our heavy woes
  To raise us to his throne;
There's not a gift his hand bestows
  But cost his heart a groan.

January

25. Because thine heart was tender, and thou hast humbled thyself before the LORD.—2 KINGS 22:19.

O for that tenderness of heart
  Which bows before the Lord;
Acknowledges how just thou art,
  And trembles at thy word!

---

26. And ye shall be hated of all men for my name's sake.—MATT. 10:22.

If on my face, for thy dear name,
  Shame and reproaches be,
All hail reproach, and welcome shame,
  If thou rememb'rst me.

January

27. Make me to hear joy and gladness; that the bones which thou hast broken may rejoice.—Psa. 51:8.

Give my dejected soul to prove
   The joy of thy forgiving love;
Pour balm into my bleeding breast,
   And lead my weary feet to rest.

---

28. I am thine, save me; for I have sought thy precepts.—Psa. 119:94.

Teach my weak heart, O gracious Lord,
   With stronger faith to call thee mine;
Bid me pronounce the blissful word,
   My Father, God, with joy divine.

January

29. Because thy lovingkindness is better than life, my lips shall praise thee.

—Psa. 63:3.

When trouble, like a gloomy cloud,
  Has gathered thick and thundered loud,
He near my soul has always stood—
  His lovingkindness, oh how good!

---

30. Thou art the same, and thy years shall not fail.—Heb. 1:12.

No change of mind our Jesus knows,
  A true and constant friend!
When once the Lord his love bestows,
  He loves unto the end.

January

31. Through him we both have access by one Spirit unto the Father.—Eph. 2:18.

In Christ, our medium of access,
    We've pardon, rest, and righteousness
The Father draws, the Spirit seals,
    And everlasting life reveals.

February

1. He will not fail thee, neither forsake thee: fear not, neither be dismayed.

—DEUT. 31:8.

Then let the Lord for ever reign,
    And sway us as he will;
Sick or in health, in ease or pain,
    We are his people still.

---

2. To them gave he power to become the sons of God, even to them that believe on his name.—JOHN 1:12.

Salvation in that name is found,
    Balm of my grief and care;
A med'cine for my every wound,
    All, all I want is there.

February

3. He that is joined unto the Lord is one spirit.—1 COR. 6:17.

To Jesus joined, we all that's good
    From him our Head derive;
We eat his flesh, and drink his blood,
    And *by* and *in* him live.

---

4. Who hath also sealed us, and given the earnest of the Spirit in our hearts.

—2 COR. 1:22.

Come, Holy Ghost, all-quickening fire,
    Come, and in me delight to rest;
Grant the supplies that I require:
    O come, and consecrate my breast!

February

5. He that loveth not knoweth not God;
for God is love.—1 JOHN 4:8.

His sympathies to Israel's race
    In sweet compassions move;
He clothes his looks with softest grace,
    And takes his title—LOVE.

---

6. Who is gone into heaven, and is on
the right hand of God.—1 PET. 3:22.

Now though he reigns exalted high,
    His love is still as great;
Well he remembers Calvary,
    Nor let our souls forget.

February

7. And came and preached peace to you which were afar off, and to them that were nigh.—EPH. 2:17.

> Then if thine eye of faith be dim,
>   Rest thou on Jesus, sink or swim;
> And at his footstool bow thy knee,—
>   His precious blood thy peace shall be.

---

8. They that be whole need not a physician, but they that are sick.

—MATT. 9:12.

> See in the Saviour's dying blood
>   Life, health, and bliss abundant flow!
> 'Tis only this dear sacred flood
>   Can ease thy pain and heal thy woe.

February

9. When Jesus therefore had received the vinegar, he said, It is finished.

—JOHN 19:30.

Justice was *fully* satisfied,
　Atonement *fully* made;
The law was *fully* magnified,
　And wondrous love displayed.

---

10. Thou hast been my defence and refuge in the day of my trouble.

—PSA. 59:16.

In every trouble, sharp and strong,
　My soul to Jesus flies;
My anchor-hold is firm in him
　When swelling billows rise.

February

11. Christ also hath loved us, and hath given himself for us.—Eph. 5:2.

> For us the Saviour's blood avails,
>   Almighty to atone;
> The hands he gave to piercing nails
>   Shall lead us to his throne.

---

12. The Holy Ghost, whom the Father will send in my name, he shall teach you all things.—John 14:26.

> He quickens the dead by the word of his grace,
>   He opens the eyes of the blind,
> Then leads to the Saviour for pardon and peace,
>   And blessings of every kind.

February

13. I will hope continually, and will yet praise thee more and more.—Psa. 71:14.

> In all our troubles may we wait,
>   And meekly kiss the rod;
> Deliverance never comes too late
>   To those who hope in God.

---

14. The desire of our soul is to thy name, and to the remembrance of thee.

—Isa. 26:8.

> Deliverance to my soul proclaim,
>   And life and liberty;
> Show forth the virtue of thy name,
>   And Jesus prove to me.

February

15. Serving the Lord with all humility of mind.—ACTS 20:19.

Humility the Lord beholds
　　With an approving eye;
In humble souls he doth delight,
　　For such on him rely.

---

16. Where sin abounded, grace did much more abound.—ROM. 5:20.

The vilest of sinners forgiveness have found,
　　For Jesus was humbled that grace might
　　　　abound;
Whoever repents of his sin against God
　　Shall surely be pardoned through Calvary's
　　　　blood.

February

17. Behold my servant, whom I uphold;
mine elect, in whom my soul delighteth.

—ISA. 42:1.

Jesus, in condescending love,
    Thus makes his grace appear;
He left the shining realms above
    To be a servant here.

---

18. And when they had nothing to pay,
he frankly forgave them both.

—LUKE 7:42.

'Tis perfect poverty alone
    That sets the soul at large;
While we can call one mite our own
    We have no full discharge.

February

19. Rest in the LORD, and wait patiently for him.—PSA. 37:7.

> O for that sweet simplicity
>   That rests alone on Christ;
> Just like as helpless infancy
>   Hangs on the mother's breast.

---

20. My kindness shall not depart from thee, neither shall the covenant of my peace be removed.—ISA. 54:10.

> Firm as his throne his covenant stands;
>   Though earth should shake and skies depart,
> You're safe in your Redeemer's hands,
>   Who bears your name upon his heart.

February

21. We which have believed do enter into rest.—HEB. 4:3.

> By Christ we enter into rest,
>   And triumph o'er the fall;
> Whoe'er would be completely blest
>   Must trust to Christ for all.

22. And when he was in affliction, he besought the LORD his God, and humbled himself greatly.—2 CHRON. 33:12.

> Afflictions, though they seem severe,
>   In mercy oft are sent;
> They show the prodigal his sin,
>   And lead him to repent.

February

23. Commit thy way unto the LORD; trust also in him; and he shall bring it to pass.—PSA. 37:5.

> O might I doubt no more,
>   But in his pleasure rest,
> Whose wisdom, love, and truth, and power
>   Engage to make me blest.

---

24. Without controversy great is the mystery of godliness: God was manifest in the flesh.—1 TIM. 3:16.

> Almighty God sighed human breath!
>   The Lord of life experienced death!
> How it was done we can't discuss,
>   But this we know, 'twas done for us.

February

25. So have I sworn that I will not be wroth with thee, nor rebuke thee.

—Isa. 54:9.

Though darkness spread around our tent,
  Though fear prevail and joy decline,
God will not of his oath repent;
  Dear Lord, thy people still are thine!

_____

26. If ye through the Spirit do mortify the deeds of the body, ye shall live.

—Rom. 8:13.

Jesus, my life, thyself apply,
  Thine hallowing Spirit breathe;
My vile affections crucify;
  Conform me to thy death.

February

27. God imputeth righteousness without works.—Rom. 4:6.

> Imputed righteousness alone
>   Can bring the guilty nigh;
> Give boldness at Jehovah's throne,
>   And right to joys on high.

---

28. He was received up into heaven, and sat on the right hand of God.

—Mark 16:19.

> What can Christians have to fear,
>   When they view their Saviour there?
> Hell is vanquished, heaven appeased,
>   God is reconciled and pleased.

February

29. Him hath God exalted with his right hand to be a Prince and a Saviour, for to give repentance.—Acts 5:31.

The Lamb is exalted repentance to give,
  That sin may be hated, while sinners believe;
Contrition is granted, and God justified,
  The sinner is humbled, and self is denied.

March

1. Have mercy upon me, O LORD; for I am weak.—PSA. 6:2.

> I'm helpless as a little child,
>   And like it I would rest;
> Show me, O God, a parent's heart.
>   Give me an infant's trust.

---

2. Rejoice in Christ Jesus, and have no confidence in the flesh.—PHIL. 3:3.

> Whatever be thy frame,
>   Though dull and cold as ice,
> No change has taken place in him;
>   Then in the Lord rejoice.

March

3. The LORD will give grace and glory.
—PSA. 84:11.

Oh may I practically show
   My interest in thy grace;
Be all I am, and have, and do,
   Devoted to thy praise.

4. In all things it behoved him to be
made like unto his brethren.—HEB. 2:17.

Christ, your fellow-sufferer, see,
   He was in all things like to you:
Are you tempted? so was he;
   Deserted? he was too.

March

5. By the obedience of one shall many be made righteous.—ROM. 5:19.

> Though hellish smoke my duty stain,
>   And sin deform me quite,
> The blood of Jesus makes me clean,
>   And his obedience white.

---

6. After ye were illuminated, ye endured a great fight of afflictions.—HEB. 10:32.

> Many and great our trials are,
>   But every trial we shall bear,
> While we the word of God regard,
>   And cast our burdens on the Lord.

March

7. I said not unto the seed of Jacob, Seek ye me in vain.—ISA. 45:19.

> Then wait, my soul, upon the Lord,
>   Believe, and ask again;
> Thou hast his kind and faithful word,
>   That none shall ask in vain.

———

8. It is the voice of my beloved that knocketh, saying, Open to me, my sister, my love.—SONG OF SOL. 5:2.

> Come quickly in, thou heavenly guest.
>   Nor ever hence remove,
> But sup with me, and let the feast
>   Be everlasting love.

March

9. Casting all your care upon him; for he careth for you.—1 PET. 5:7.

> To Jesus look, thy cares forego,
>   All earth-born cares are wrong;
> Man wants but little here below,
>   Nor wants that little long.

———

10. Truly our fellowship is with the Father, and with his Son Jesus Christ.

—1 JOHN 1:3.

> With God sweet converse I maintain;
>   Great as he is, I dare be free;
> I tell him all my grief and pain,
>   And he reveals his love to me.

March

11. The LORD trieth the righteous.

—PSA. 11:5.

Trials may press of every sort,
    They may be sore, they must be short:
We now believe, but soon shall view,
    The greatest glories God can show.

------

12. Let him take hold of my strength,
that he may make peace with me.

—ISA. 27:5.

Could I of thy strength take hold,
    And always feel thee near,
Confident, divinely bold,
    My soul should scorn to fear.

March

13. The very God of peace sanctify you wholly.—1 THESS. 5:23.

Rule in me, Lord, my foes control,
　　Which would not own thy sway;
Diffuse thy likeness through my soul,
　　Shine to the perfect day.

———

14. Examine me, O LORD, and prove me; try my reins and my heart.—PSA. 26:2.

Since all my secret ways
　　Are marked and known to thee,
Afford me, Lord, thy light of grace,
　　That I myself may see.

March

15. The LORD God is a sun and shield.
                              —PSA. 84:11.

Let not my hopes be overcast
    With shadows of despair;
Dart through my soul thy quick'ning beam,
    And shine for ever there.

---

16. The LORD will strengthen him upon the bed of languishing.—PSA. 41:3.

Jesus shall be thy helping friend,
    Thy good physician, nay, thy nurse;
To make thy bed shall condescend,
    And from the affliction take the curse.

March

17. Cleanse thou me from secret faults.

—Psa. 19:12.

O cleanse me in a Saviour's blood,
   Transform me by thy power,
And make me thy beloved abode,
   And let me rove no more.

———

18. And being in an agony he prayed more earnestly.—Luke 22:44.

If thou of murmuring must be cured,
   Compare thy griefs with mine;
Think what my love for thee endured,
   And thou wilt not repine.

March

19. LORD, lift up the light of thy countenance upon us.—PSA. 4:6.

> Lift up thy countenance serene,
>   And let thy happy child
> Behold, without a cloud between,
>   The Father reconciled.

---

20. He was wounded for our transgressions, he was bruised for our iniquities.
—ISA. 53:5.

> That dear blood, for sinners spilt,
>   Shows my sin in all its guilt;
> Ah! my soul, he bore thy load—
>   Thou hast slain the Lamb of God.

March

21. I am Alpha and Omega, the first and the last.—Rev. 1:11.

All the names that love could find,
    All the forms that love could take,
Jesus in himself hath joined,
    Thee, my soul, his own to make.

———

22. Thou shalt fear the Lord thy God; him shalt thou serve, and to him shalt thou cleave.—Deut. 10:20.

Should I from thee, my God, remove,
    Life could no lasting bliss afford:
My joy, the sense of pard'ning love;
    My guard, the presence of my Lord.

March

23. I have waited for thy salvation, O
LORD.—GEN. 49:18.

> Give us quietly to tarry
>   Till for all thy glory meet—
> Waiting, like attentive Mary,
>   Happy at the Saviour's feet.

---

24. I find then a law, that, when I would
do good, evil is present with me.

—ROM. 7:21.

> Far worse than all my foes I find
>   The enemy within—
> The evil heart, the carnal mind—
>   Mine own insidious sin.

March

25. Ye have overcome the wicked one.

—1 John 2:13.

Lord, bring me to this glorious end!
    And from this heart of mine,
Oh, drive and keep away the fiend
    Who fears no voice but thine.

---

26. If children, then heirs; heirs of God
and joint-heirs with Christ.—Rom. 8:17.

Come, then, my God, mark out thine heir:
    Of heaven a larger earnest give!
With clearer light thy witness bear—
    More sensibly within me live.

March

27. O Lord, I am oppressed; undertake for me.—Isa. 38:14.

> God knows the pains his servants feel,
>   He hears his children cry;
> To help in weakness and in want
>   His grace is ever nigh.

---

28. Blessed is the man whom thou chastenest, O LORD, and teachest him out of thy law.—Psa. 94:12.

> 'Tis good that saints should trust the Lord,
>   And seek for comfort in his Word;
> There all they read will tend to prove
>   That their afflictions are in love.

March

29. Peace I leave with you, my peace I give unto you.—JOHN 14:27.

> The peace which man can ne'er conceive,
> The love and joy unknown,
> Now, Saviour, to thy servant give,
> And claim me for thine own.

———

30. For yet a little while, and he that shall come will come, and will not tarry.
—HEB. 10:37.

> A few more days, or months, or years,
> In this dark desert to complain;
> A few more sighs, a few more tears,
> And we shall bid adieu to pain.

March

31. Greater is he that is in you, than he that is in the world.—1 JOHN 4:4.

Through seas of blood and fields of death
　　We march with dauntless courage on—
Immortal, till God takes our breath;
　　Immortal, till our work is done.

✠

April

1. Thou standest by faith. Be not high-minded, but fear.—ROM. 11:20.

> Trust the Lord in life and death,
>   Trust your all in Jesus' hand;
> Trust him with your latest breath,
>   For by faith alone you stand.

————

2. Who is he that will harm you, if ye be followers of that which is good?

—1 PET. 3:13.

> Though I am weak and Satan strong,
>   And often to assault me tries,
> When Jesus is my shield and song,
>   Abashed the foe before me flies.

April

3. All things are for your sakes.

—2 Cor. 4:15.

All things for our good are given,
  Comforts, crosses, staffs, or rods;
All is ours in earth and heaven—
  We are Christ's, and Christ is God's.

---

4. By his knowledge shall my righteous servant justify many; for he shall bear their iniquities.—Isa. 53:11.

God our sins imputes to him,
  Imputes to us his righteousness;
Guilty he doth Christ esteem,
  And guiltless us confess.

April

5. We walk by faith, not by sight.

—2 COR 5:7.

> Oh, may I learn, in every state,
>   To make his will my own;
> And when the joys of sense depart,
>   To walk by faith alone.

---

6. I am troubled; I am bowed down greatly; I go mourning all the day long.

—PSA. 38:6.

> When trials vex my doubting mind,
>   Jesus, to thee I'll flee;
> No shelter can I elsewhere find,
>   No refuge but in thee.

April

7. Lay up for yourselves treasures in heaven.—MATT. 6:20.

With anxious care let others press
To read their worldly fate;
I only for assurance wish
Of my celestial state.

---

8. Thou hast played the harlot with many lovers; yet return again to me, saith the LORD.—JER. 3:1.

Oh, wash me in the Saviour's blood,
Transform me by thy power,
And seal me thy beloved abode,
And let me rove no more!

April

9. Forgetting those things which are behind, and reaching forth unto those things which are before.—PHIL. 3:13.

Supported by thy changeless love,
   I tend to realms of peace,
Where every sorrow shall remove,
   And every sin shall cease.

---

10. Be silent, O all flesh, before the LORD.

—ZECH. 2:13.

Then turn thee to thy rest, my soul,
   And kiss the needful rod;
Nor seek thy Sovereign to control,
   But know that he is God.

April

11. Whatsoever ye do in word or deed, do all in the name of the Lord Jesus.

—Col. 3:17.

Be all my heart, be all my days,
  Devoted to thy single praise!
And let my glad obedience prove
  How much I owe, how much I love.

———————

12. The things which are not seen are eternal.—2 Cor. 4:18.

Thanks for mercies past receive;
  Pardon of my sins renew;
Teach me henceforth how to live
  With eternity in view.

April

13. O LORD, thou art our father; we are the clay, and thou our potter.—ISA. 64:8.

My potter from above,
  Clay in thy hands I am;
Mould me into obedient love,
  And stamp me with thy name.

————

14. Wash me, and I shall be whiter than snow.—PSA. 51:7.

Wash me, and seal me for thine own;
  Wash me, and mine thou art;
Wash me, but not my feet alone—
  My hands, my head, my heart.

April

15. Weeping may endure for a night, but joy cometh in the morning.—Psa. 30:5.

Though God may delay to show us his light,
    And heaviness may endure for a night,
Yet joy in the morning shall surely abound;
    No shadow of turning in Jesus is found.

———

16. My son, despise not thou the chastening of the Lord.—Heb. 12:5.

Had I but knowledge to discern
    Thy wisdom, love, and power,
From every sorrow I should learn
    To thank thee more and more.

April

17. Thou gavest also thy good spirit to instruct them.—NEH. 9:20.

Thy Spirit, O God, in me shed abroad,
    And show me my interest in Jesus' blood;
Then, then shall I prove thy peace from above,
    And fly to thy throne on the wings of thy love.

---

18. The LORD is the portion of my inheritance and of my cup.—PSA. 16:5.

Thy gifts, O Lord, cannot suffice,
    Unless thyself be given;
Thy presence makes my paradise—
    Where'er thou art is heaven.

19. That in the ages to come he might shew the exceeding riches of his grace in his kindness toward us.

—Eph. 2:7.

'Twas grace that quickened me when dead,
'Twas grace my soul to Jesus led;
Grace brings a sense of pardoned sin,
And grace subdues my lusts within.

———

20. O keep my soul, and deliver me.

—Psa. 25:20.

Keep me safe from all delusion,
Well protected from all harms,
Free from sin and all confusion,—
Circle me within thy arms.

April

21. God sent his only begotten Son into the world, that we might live through him.—1 John 4:9.

> Such was the pity of our God,
>   He loved the race of man so well,
> He sent his Son to bear our load
>   Of sins, and save our souls from hell.

---

22. Turn you to the strong hold, ye prisoners of hope.—Zech. 9:12.

> O Jesus, to thee I turn me for aid,
>   Whose mercy for me atonement hath made;
> Accept of me freely, thy love shed abroad,
>   And let me now feel thee my Saviour and God.

April

23. My covenant will I not break, nor alter the thing that is gone out of my lips.—PSA. 89:34.

The Lord will scourge us if we stray,
    And wound us with distress;
But he will never take away
    His covenant of peace.

---

24. The desire of all nations shall come.
    —HAG. 2:7.

Yes, Jesus, thou art our desire,
    In thee our wishes meet;
Nor can the whole creation round
    Afford a name so sweet.

April

25. That we should be to the praise of his glory, who first trusted in Christ.

—Eph. 1:12.

What are my works but sin and death,
　Till God his quickening Spirit breathe!
In nothing will I trust beside
　The finished work of him who died.

---

26. O Lord, how manifold are thy works! in wisdom hast thou made them all.—Psa. 104:24.

In all our Maker's grand designs
　Omnipotence with wisdom shines;
His works through all this wondrous frame
　Bear the great impress of his name.

April

27. The LORD is good unto them that wait for him, to the soul that seeketh him.—LAM. 3:25.

> He listens to my low complaints,
> Enlivens all my mourning days,
> Revives my spirit when it faints,
> And turns my faltering voice to praise.

---

28. Your Father knoweth what things ye have need of, before ye ask him.

—MATT. 6:8.

> Our Father knows what's good and fit,
> And wisdom guides his love:
> To his appointments we submit,
> And every choice approve.

April

29. Wherefore doth a living man complain, a man for the punishment of his sins?—LAM. 3:39.

> Whate'er thy sacred will ordains,
> Oh, give me strength to bear;
> And let me know my Father reigns,
> And trust his tender care.

---

30. They shall never perish, neither shall any man pluck them out of my hand.

—JOHN 10:28.

> Thou my fortress art and tower;
> Having thee, I want no more:
> Strong in thy full strength I stand;
> None can pluck me from thy hand.

May

1. The works of the LORD are great,
sought out of all them that have pleasure therein.—PSA. 111:2.

Oh, may my soul with rapture trace
　Thy works of nature and of grace;
Explore thy sacred name, and still
　Press on to know and do thy will!

2. It is good that a man should both
hope and quietly wait for the salvation
of the LORD.—LAM. 3:26.

My God, my Father, be thy name
　My solace and my stay;
In mercy seal my humble claim,
　And drive my fears away.

May

3. The Lord is nigh unto them that are
of a broken heart; and saveth such as be
of a contrite spirit.—PSA. 34:18.

> To calm the sorrows of the mind,
>   Our heavenly Friend is nigh;
> To wipe the anxious tear that starts
>   Or trembles in the eye.

---

4. Then Jesus said unto the twelve, Will
ye also go away?—JOHN 6:67.

> To go away from thee!
>   What sin and folly worse?
> Who from a smiling God would flee,
>   To meet a frowning curse?

May

5. Whom have I in heaven but thee? and there is none upon earth that I desire beside thee.—Psa. 73:25.

All my treasure is above,
  All my riches is thy love.
Who the worth of love can tell?
  Infinite! unsearchable!

---

6. The gifts and calling of God are without repentance.—Rom. 11:29.

Lord, let not groundless fears destroy
  The mercies now possessed:
I'll praise for blessings I enjoy,
  And trust for all the rest.

May

7. A man shall be as a hiding place from the wind, and a covert from the tempest.
—Isa. 32:2.

> Save me from the furious blast;
>   A covert from the tempest be;
> Hide me, Jesus, till o'erpast
>   The storm of sin I see.

---

8. Blessed is that man that maketh the Lord his trust.—Psa. 40:4.

> He will perform the work begun;
>   Jesus, the sinner's Friend,
> Jesus, the Lover of his own,
>   Will love me to the end.

May

9. He restoreth my soul: he leadeth me in the paths of righteousness for his name's sake.—Psa. 23:3.

> He brings my wandering spirit back,
>   When I forsake his ways;
> And leads me, for his mercy's sake,
>   In paths of truth and grace.

---

10. He that humbleth himself shall be exalted.—Luke 14:11.

> Is not haughtiness of heart
>   The gulf between my God and me?
> Meek Redeemer, now impart
>   Thine own humility.

May

11. If ye endure chastening, God dealeth with you as with sons.—HEB. 12:7.

Did I meet no trials here,
  No chastisement by the way,
Might I not with reason fear
  I should prove a castaway?

———

12. In God have I put my trust: I will not be afraid what man can do unto me.

—PSA. 56:11.

No longer let me be afraid;
  The promise shall take place:
His strength's in weakness perfect made;
  Sufficient is his grace.

May

13. Whosoever doth not bear his cross, and come after me, cannot be my disciple.—LUKE 14:27.

> For ever here my rest shall be,
>   Close to thy bleeding side;
> This all my hope and all my pleas,
>   For me the Saviour died.

---

14. The LORD also will be a refuge for the oppressed, a refuge in times of trouble.—PSA. 9:9.

> Other refuge have I none;
>   Hangs my helpless soul on thee:
> Leave, oh, leave me not alone,
>   Still support and comfort me!

May

15. Who was delivered for our offences, and was raised again for our justification.—Rom. 4:25.

When from the dust of death I rise
    To take my mansion in the skies,
Even then shall this be all my plea,—
    'Jesus hath lived and died for me.'

---

16. Having food and raiment let us be therewith content.—1 Tim. 6:8.

Give me a calm, a thankful heart,
    From every murmur free;
The blessings of thy grace impart,
    And make me live to thee.

May

17. As many as are led by the Spirit of God, they are the sons of God.

—ROM 8:14.

Lead me to God, my final rest,
   In his enjoyment to be blest;
Lead me to heaven, the seat of bliss,
   Where pleasure in perfection is.

18. A new heart also will I give you, and a new spirit will I put within you.

—EZEK. 36:26.

Give me a heart resigned and meek,
   My dear Redeemer's throne;
Where only Christ is heard to speak,
   Where Jesus reigns alone.

19. We also joy in God through our Lord Jesus Christ, by whom we have now received the atonement.—Rom. 5:11.

Who in heart on thee believes,
    He the atonement now receives;
He with joy beholds thy face,
    Triumphs in thy pard'ning grace.

———

20. Come now, and let us reason together, saith the Lord.—Isa. 1:18.

Arise, my soul, from deep distress,
    And banish every fear;
He calls thee to his throne of grace,
    To spread thy sorrows there.

May

21. The Lord shall deliver me from every evil work, and will preserve me unto his heavenly kingdom.—2 Tim. 4:18.

Jesus the Lord shall guard me safe
   From every ill design;
And to his heavenly kingdom keep
   This feeble soul of mine.

————

22. Shall we continue in sin, that grace may abound?—Rom. 6:1.

Lord, let me not thy grace abuse,
   And sin because thou'rt good;
But fill my inmost soul with shame
   That I thy love withstood.

23. Behold, he that keepeth Israel shall neither slumber nor sleep.—Psa. 121:4.

Be my guide in every peril,
  Watch me hourly night and day;
Else my foolish heart will wander
  From thy Spirit far away.

---

24. Thou hast destroyed thyself; but in me is thine help.—Hos. 13:9.

Jesus, in whom the Godhead's rays
  Beam forth with mildest majesty,
I see thee full of truth and grace,
  And come for all I want to thee.

May

25. Our help is in the name of the LORD, who made heaven and earth.

—PSA. 124:8.

If rough and thorny be the way,
  My strength proportion to my day;
Till toil, and grief, and pain shall cease,
  Where all is rest, and joy, and peace.

---

26. The love of Christ constraineth us.

—2 COR. 5:14.

When shall thy love constrain
  This heart thine own to be?
When shall the wounded spirit gain
  A healing rest in thee?

May

27. The Spirit itself beareth witness with our spirit, that we are the children of God.—Rom. 8:16.

> Assure my conscience of her part
>   In the Redeemer's blood,
> And bear thy witness with my heart
>   That I am born of God.

---

28. Being then made free from sin, ye became the servants of righteousness.

—Rom. 6:18.

> On me, my King, exert thy power,
>   Make old things pass away;
> Transform and draw my soul to thee
>   Still nearer every day.

May

29. He humbled himself, and became obedient unto death, even the death of the cross.—PHIL. 2:8.

My worthless heart to gain,
　The God who gave me breath
Was found in fashion as a man,
　And died a cursed death.

---

30. The LORD is nigh unto all them that call upon him, to all that call upon him in truth.—PSA. 145:18.

Jesus, thou didst shed thy blood;
　On this rock our hope we raise.
Thou hast brought us nigh to God;
　Thine the work and thine the praise.

May

31. I exercise myself, to have always a conscience void of offence toward God, and toward men.—ACTS 24:16.

I want a principle within
    Of jealous, godly fear;
A tender sense of rising sin,
    A pain to feel it near.

June

1. Oh, do not this abominable thing that I hate.—JER. 44:4.

May I from every sin,
    As from a serpent, fly;
Abhor to touch the thing unclean,
    And rather choose to die.

———

2. Behold, I have given him for a leader and commander to the people.

—ISA. 55:4.

Behold, he leads the way;
    We'll follow where he goes:
We cannot fail to win the day,
    Since he subdues our foes.

June

3. When wilt thou comfort me?

—Psa. 119:82.

Lord, let me hear thy pardoning voice,
    And make my troubled soul rejoice!
Then all my powers shall join to bless
    The Lord, my strength and righteousness.

---

4. The law of thy mouth is better unto
me than thousands of gold and silver.

—Psa. 119:72.

Oh, may the least omission pain
    My well-instructed soul,
And drive me to the blood again,
    Which makes the wounded whole.

June

5. I will guide thee with mine eye.

—Psa. 32:8.

Are we blind and prone to error?
  God vouchsafes to be our guide:
Are we faint and full of terror?
  He himself is on our side.

———————

6. It is an evil thing and bitter, that thou
has forsaken the Lord thy God.

—Jer. 2:19.

From thee that I no more may part,
  No more thy goodness grieve,
The filial awe, the holy heart,
  The tender conscience give.

June

7. All men forsook me; notwithstanding the Lord stood with me.

—2 Tim. 4:16, 17.

Friends may fail, but he will take you
  And supply your utmost need;
Nor will Jesus e'er forsake you,
  But in paths of safety lead.

---

8. If we suffer, we shall also reign with him: if we deny him, he also will deny us.—2 Tim. 2:12.

Lord, we expect to suffer here;
  Nor would we dare repine;
But give us still to find thee near,
  And own us still for thine.

June

9. I will instruct thee and teach thee in the way which thou shalt go.—PSA. 32:8.

With confidence I seek thy face,
  Thy gracious promise, Lord, fulfil;
And grant me light, and grant me grace,
  To know and do thy perfect will.

———

10. Watch and pray, that ye enter not into temptation.—MATT. 26:41.

Whene'er temptations fright my heart,
  Or lure my feet aside,
My God, thy powerful aid impart,
  My guardian and my guide.

June

11. Take heed, brethren, lest there be in any of you an evil heart of unbelief.

—HEB. 3:12.

Lord, with this guilty heart of mine
 To thy dear cross I flee;
And to thy grace my soul resign,
 To be renewed by thee.

---

12. What is your life? It is even a vapour.

—JAMES 4:14.

My days are shorter than a span—
 A little point my life appears;
How frail, at best, is dying man!
 How vain are all his hopes and fears!

June

13. Create in me a clean heart, O God; and renew a right spirit within me.

—PSA. 51:10.

Do thou my sins subdue,
  Thy sovereign love make known;
The spirit of my mind renew,
  And save me in thy Son.

---

14. Worship the LORD in the beauty of holiness.—1 CHRON. 16:29.

The deepest reverence of the mind,
  Pay, O my soul, to God;
Lift with thy hands a holy heart
  To his sublime abode.

June

15. He shall come to be glorified in his saints, and to be admired in all them that believe.—2 Thess. 1:10.

O glorious hour! O blest abode!
  I shall be near and like my God!
And flesh and sin no more control
  The sacred pleasures of the soul.

---

16. When he is tried, he shall receive the crown of life.—James 1:12.

Then why, my soul, complain or fear?
  The crown of glory see!
The more I toil and suffer here,
  The sweeter rest will be.

June

17. Who is like unto thee, O Lord, glorious in holiness, fearful in praises, doing wonders?—Exod. 15:11.

Who can behold the blazing light?
    Who can approach consuming flame?
None but thy Wisdom knows thy might,
    None but thy Word can speak thy name.

---

18. Forbearing one another, and forgiving one another.—Col. 3:13.

I hope for pardon, through thy Son,
    For all the crimes which I have done;
Oh, may the grace that pardons me
    Constrain me to forgive like thee.

June

19. For the flesh lusteth against the Spirit, and the Spirit against the flesh.

—GAL. 5:17.

How long, dear Saviour, shall I feel
   These struggles in my breast?
When wilt thou bow my stubborn will,
   And give my conscience rest?

---

20. He will magnify the law, and make it honourable.—ISA. 42:21.

Here I behold thy wonders, Lord!
   How Christ hath to thy law restored
Those honours, on the atoning day,
   Which guilty sinners took away.

June

21. Consider him that endured such contradiction of sinners against himself.
—HEB. 12:3.

My soul rejoices to pursue
   The steps of him I love;
Till glory break upon my view,
   In brighter worlds above.

---

22. The word of our God shall stand for ever.—ISA. 40:8.

May this blest volume ever lie
   Close to my heart, and near my eye,
Till life's last hour my soul engage,
   And be my chosen heritage!

June

23. Thy word is a lamp unto my feet, and a light unto my path.—Psa. 119:105.

> Oh, may these heavenly pages be
>   My ever dear delight;
> And still new beauties may I see,
>   And still increasing light!

24. Father, forgive them; for they know what they do.—Luke 23:34.

> Hark, how he prays! (the charming sound
>   Dwells on his dying lips), 'Forgive!'
> And every groan and gaping wound
>   Cries, 'Father, let the rebels live!'

June

25. He is able also to save them to the uttermost that come unto God by him.

—Heb. 7:25.

Our Jesus saves from sin and hell;
  His words are true and sure,
And on this rock our faith may rest
  Immovably secure.

---

26. The mercy of the Lord is from ever-lasting to everlasting upon them that fear him.—Psa. 103:17.

His sovereign mercy knows no end,
  His faithfulness shall still endure;
And those who on his word depend
  Shall find his word of promise sure.

June

27. I have called you friends; for all things that I have heard of my Father I have made known unto you.

—JOHN 15:15.

> He calls a worm his friend!
>   He calls himself my God!
> And he shall save me to the end.
>   Through his own blood.

———

28. The LORD will perfect that which concerneth me.—PSA. 138:8.

> Grace will complete what grace begins,
>   To save from sorrows and from sins:
> The work that wisdom undertakes
>   Eternal mercy ne'er forsakes.

29. He hath clothed me with the garments of salvation, he hath covered me with the robe of righteousness.

—Isa. 61:10.

This spotless robe the same appears
    When ruined nature sinks in years:
No age can change its glorious hue;
    The robe of Christ is ever new.

---

30. Strengthen thou me according unto thy word.—Psa. 119:28.

Pity my frailty, dearest Lord;
    Grace in the needful hour afford:
O steel this timorous heart of mine
    With fortitude and love divine.

July

1. Christ is the end of the law for righteousness to every one that believeth.

—ROM. 10:4.

To see the law by Christ fulfilled,
  And hear his pardoning voice,
Changes a slave into a child,
  And duty into choice.

---

2. I am not ashamed of the gospel of Christ: for it is the power of God unto salvation to every one that believeth.

—ROM. 1:16.

Here Jesus in ten thousand ways
  His soul-attracting charms displays;
Recounts his poverty and pains,
  And tells his love in melting strains.

July

3. Whosoever he be of you that forsaketh not all that he hath, he cannot be my disciple.—LUKE 14:33.

I all on earth forsake,
  Its wisdom, fame, and power:
And him my only portion make,
  My shield and tower.

---

4. Wait on the LORD: be of good courage, and he shall strengthen thine heart.—PSA. 27:14.

Wait, O believer, on the Lord,
  And rest with courage on his word;
Wait, for his arm will strength impart,
  Till endless triumph glad your heart.

July

5. He shall gather the lambs with his arm, and carry them in his bosom.

—ISA. 40:11.

> Jesus, Shepherd of thy sheep,
>   Gather me within thy arms;
> Safely in thy bosom keep,
>   Free from dangers and alarms.

---

6. Thou saidst, There is no hope: no; for I have loved strangers, and after them will I go.—JER. 2:25.

> Does he want slaves to grace his throne,
>   Or rules he by an iron rod?
> Loves he the deep despairing groan—
>   To be a tyrant, or a God?

July

7. Remember me, O Lord, with the favour that thou bearest unto thy people.

—Psa. 106:4.

Their daily wants his hands supply;
  Their steps he guards with watchful eye;
Leads them from earth to heaven above,
  And crowns them with eternal love.

---

8. Thou wast slain, and hast redeemed us to God by thy blood.—Rev. 5:9.

When sinners broke the Father's laws,
  The dying Son atones;
Oh, the dear mysteries of his cross!
  The triumph of his groans!

July

9. Behold, what manner of love the Father hath bestowed upon us, that we should be called the sons of God.

—1 JOHN 3:1.

> To us the privilege is given,
>   To be the sons and heirs of heaven,
> Sons of the God that reigns on high,
>   And heirs of God beyond the sky.

———————

10. Let integrity and uprightness preserve me.—PSA. 25:21.

> Be thou my all-sufficient friend,
>   Till all my toils shall cease;
> Guard me through life, and let my end,
>   Be everlasting peace.

July

11. Nor any other creature, shall be able to separate us from the love of God, which is in Christ Jesus our Lord.

—Rom. 8:39.

Things future, nor things that are now,
  Not all things below or above,
Can make him his purpose forego,
  Or sever my soul from his love.

———————

12. Is this thy kindness to thy friend?

—2 Sam. 16:17.

Sure were I not most vile and base,
  I could not thus my Friend requite;
And were not he the God of grace,
  He'd frown and spurn me from his sight.

July

13. LORD, thou wilt ordain peace for us: for thou also hast wrought all our works in us.—ISA. 26:12.

> Dear Saviour, let thy love pursue
>   The gracious work it has begun;
> Each secret lurking foe subdue,
>   And let our hearts be thine alone.

---

14. For thy name's sake, O LORD, pardon mine iniquity; for it is great.—PSA. 25:11.

> Not all the sins which we have wrought
>   So much his tender bowels grieve,
> As this unkind, injurious thought,
>   That he's unwilling to forgive.

July

15. Beloved, think it not strange concerning the fiery trial which is to try you.
—1 PET. 4:12.

Trials must and will befall:
    But with humble faith to see
Love inscribed upon them all—
    This is happiness to me.

---

16. And this is the record, that God hath given to us eternal life, and this life is in his Son.—1 JOHN 5:11.

Oh, believe the record true,
    God to you his Son has given!
Ye may now be happy too—
    Find on earth the life of heaven.

July

17. To day, if ye will hear his voice, do not harden your hearts.—HEB. 4:7.

Hear while he speaks, he speaks today;
  Pray while he hears, unceasing pray;
Believe his promises, and then
  Obey while he commands. Amen.

---

18. Who died for us, that, whether we wake or sleep, we should live together with him.—1 THESS. 5:10.

To suffer in the traitors' place,
  To die for men, surprising grace!
Yet pass rebellious angels by—
  O why for men, dear Saviour, why?

July

19. The LORD openeth the eyes of the blind.—PSA. 146:8.

He opens the eyes of the blind,
  The beauty of Jesus to view;
He changes the bent of the mind,
  The glory of God to pursue.

---

20. Ye are risen with him through the faith of the operation of God.

—COL. 2:12.

Soar we now where Christ has led,
  Following our exalted Head!
Made like him, like him we rise;
  Ours the cross, the grave, the skies.

July

21. Behold, I lay in Sion a chief corner stone, elect, precious.—1 PET. 2:6.

> Thy people long this stone have tried,
>   And all the powers of hell defied;
> Floods of temptation beat in vain,—
>   Well doth this rock the house sustain.

---

22. Thou art neither cold nor hot: I would thou wert cold or hot.—REV. 3:15.

> Come, dearest Lord, thy grace impart,
>   To warm this lukewarm, stupid heart,
> Till all its powers and passions move
>   In melting grief and ardent love.

July

23. The Lord is risen indeed, and hath appeared to Simon.—LUKE 24:34.

Jesus, once numbered with the dead,
   Unseals his eyes, to sleep no more:
And ever lives their cause to plead
   For whom the pains of death he bore.

---

24. That I may see the good of thy chosen, that I may rejoice in the gladness of thy nation.—PSA. 106:5.

O may I see thy tribes rejoice,
   And aid their triumphs with my voice!
This is my glory, Lord, to be
   Joined to thy saints, and near to thee.

July

25. Whosoever will, let him take the water of life freely.—Rev. 22:17.

> Ye doubting sinners, come and try,
>   For Christ will not his grace deny;
> Then draw with joy, your vessels fill—
>   Come, draw and drink, whoever will!

---

26. God hath from the beginning chosen you to salvation through sanctification of the Spirit and belief of the truth.

—2 Thess. 2:13.

> Loved of my God, for him again
>   With love intense I'd burn:
> Chosen of thee ere time began,
>   I'd choose thee in return.

July

27. I will shew thee my faith by my works.—JAMES 2:18.

Have I that faith which looks to Christ,
   O'ercomes the world and sin,
Receives him Prophet, Priest, and King,
   And makes the conscience clean?

---

28. Behold, happy is the man whom God correcteth: therefore despise not thou the chastening of the Almighty.

—JOB 5:17.

Affliction's furnace is designed
   The Christian's character to show:
By this his graces are refined,
   And he is weaned from things below.

July

29. I will water it every moment: lest any hurt it, I will keep it night and day.

—Isa. 27:3.

Each moment watered by thy care,
    And fenced with power divine,
Fruit to eternal life shall bear
    The feeblest branch of thine.

---

30. I have blotted out, as a thick cloud, thy transgressions, and, as a cloud, thy sins.—Isa. 44:22.

Like a flood bursts o'er my soul,
    As Jesus seems to say,
'I've blotted thy transgressions out,
    I've washed thy sins away.'

July

31. They shall not be ashamed that wait
for me.—Isa. 49:23.

> Blest soul that can say, 'Christ only I seek';
>   Wait for him alway, be constant though
>   weak:
> The Lord whom thou seekest will not tarry
>   long:
>   And to him the weakest is dear as the
>   strong.

August

1. When they were come to the place, which is called Calvary, there they crucified him.—LUKE 23:33.

He that distributes crowns and thrones,
　Hangs on a tree, and bleeds and groans:
The Prince of Life resigns his breath;
　The King of Glory bows to death.

---

2. My beloved is white and ruddy, the chiefest among ten thousand.

—SONG OF SOL. 5:10.

May Jesus more precious become!
　His word be a lamp to our feet!
While we in this wilderness roam,
　Till brought in his presence to meet!

August

3. Know ye not that ye are the temple of God, and that the Spirit of God dwelleth in you?—1 COR. 3:16.

His blest renovation begun,
　　He dwells in the hearts of his saints:
Abandons his temple to none,
　　Nor e'er of his calling repents.

———————

4. Our gospel came not unto you in word only, but also in power, and in the Holy Ghost.—1 THESS. 1:5.

Whene'er to call the Saviour mine
　　With ardent wish my soul aspires,
Can it be less than power divine
　　Which animates those strong desires?

August

5. Work out your own salvation with fear and trembling.—PHIL. 2:12.

Then grant us, gracious Lord,
  Sweet influence from thy throne:
The work to be performed is ours,
  The strength is all thy own.

---

6. When I passed by thee, and looked upon thee, behold, thy time was the time of love.—EZEK. 16:8.

Lord, 'twas a time of wondrous love
  When thou didst first draw near my soul,
And by the Spirit from above
  My rising passions didst control.

August

7. Thy people shall be willing in the day of thy power.—PSA. 110:3.

The stubbornest will he can bow
    The foes that dwell in us restrain;
And none can be trodden so low,
    But he can revive them again.

---

8. Wilt thou not revive us again: that thy people may rejoice in thee?—PSA. 85:6.

Return and revive me once more
    With joys that are pure and divine:
Thy presence is what I implore;
    O grant it, and comfort is mine.

August

9. Turn you at my reproof: behold, I will pour out my spirit unto you.

—PROV. 1:23.

Let thy kind Spirit in my heart
　　For ever dwell, O God of love!
And light and heavenly peace impart—
　　Sweet earnest of the joys above.

---

10. After that ye believed, ye were sealed with that holy Spirit of promise.

—EPH. 1:13.

Oh, save me from the power of sin,
　　And seal me thine abode;
Thine image stamp, and make me shine,
　　A temple meet for God.

August

11. Your murmurings are not against us, but against the LORD.—EXOD. 16:8.

> I would submit to all thy will,
>   For thou art good and wise;
> Let every anxious thought be still,
>   Nor one faint murmur rise.

———

12. Behold, I have graven thee upon the palms of my hands.—ISA. 49:16.

> My name from the palms of his hands
>   Eternity will not erase;
> Impressed on his heart it remains
>   In marks of indelible grace.

August

13. That I might rest in the day of trouble.

—Hab. 3:16.

> Oh, that closer I could cleave
>   To thy bleeding, dying breast!
> Give me firmly to believe,
>   And to enter into rest.

---

14. I am in a great strait: let us fall now into the hand of the Lord.

—2 Sam. 24:14.

> The time of greatest straits
>   Thy chosen time has been,
> To manifest thy power is great,
>   And make thy glory seen.

August

15. The righteous also shall hold on his way.—JOB 17:9.

> Yes, I to the end shall endure,
>> As sure as the earnest is given;
> More happy, but not more secure,
>> The glorified spirits in heaven.

———

16. Return, ye backsliding children, and I will heal your backslidings.—JER. 3:22.

> Return, O wanderer, return,
>> Thy Saviour bids thy spirit live;
> Go to his bleeding feet and learn
>> How freely Jesus can forgive.

August

17. How long will this people provoke me?—Num. 14:11.

Lord, I believe! Oh, chase away
    The gloomy clouds of unbelief!
Lord, I repent! Oh, let thy ray
    Dissolve my heart in sacred grief!

---

18. But grow in grace, and in the knowledge of our Lord and Saviour Jesus Christ.—2 Pet. 3:18.

Precept and promise still unite
    To make this service our delight;
To grow in grace,—this, surely this,
    Is the transcendency of bliss.

August

19. But godliness with contentment is great gain.—1 TIM. 6:6.

Father, fix my soul on thee;
  Every evil let me flee;
Nothing want, beneath, above,—
  Happy in thy precious love.

---

20. Be not conformed to this world: but be ye transformed by the renewing of your mind.—ROM. 12:2.

Born by a new celestial birth,
  Why should we grovel here on earth?
Why grasp at transitory toys,
  So near to heaven's eternal joys?

August

21. They shall be my people, and I will be their God.—Jer. 32:38.

> All else, which we our treasure call,
>   May in one fatal moment fall;
> But what their happiness can move
>   Whom God the blessed deigns to love?

---

22. I will therefore that men pray every where, lifting up holy hands, without wrath and doubting.—1 Tim. 2:8.

> Prayer is the wingèd messenger
>   That bears our sighs from earth to heaven;
> That brings them to our Father's ear,
>   Nor thence returns till grace is given.

August

23. He that believeth and is baptized shall be saved.—MARK 16:16.

Thy mercy pardons crying sins,
    And washes out the deepest stains;
'Tis free, and to the vilest given—
    The vilest out of hell and heaven.

---

24. He that overcometh shall not be hurt of the second death.—REV. 2:11.

Rouse, rouse, my soul, and fight thy way,
    Should earth and hell oppose;
Though thou art not, thy Saviour is
    A match for all thy foes.

August

25. Thou shalt love the LORD thy God with all thine heart.—DEUT. 6:5.

Whate'er my foolish wandering heart,
   Attracted by a creature's power,
Would from this blissful centre start,
   Lord, fix it there to stray no more!

---

26. When my father and my mother forsake me, then the LORD will take me up.—PSA. 27:10.

Should every earthly friend depart,
   And nature leave a parent's heart,
My God, on whom my hopes depend,
   Will be my Father and my Friend.

August

27. Fear not, neither be discouraged.
—DEUT. 1:21.

> You in his wisdom, power, and love,
> May confidently trust;
> His wisdom guides, his power protects,
> His grace rewards the just.

---

28. Be ye doers of the word, and not hearers only, deceiving your own selves.—JAMES 1:22.

> In vain religion we profess
> While we reject the Lord's command:
> Strangers to God and happiness,
> We build our house upon the sand.

August

29. The LORD giveth wisdom.

—PROV. 2:6.

Happy the man who finds the grace,
   The blessing of God's chosen race;
The wisdom coming from above,
   And faith that sweetly works by love.

———————

30. Help us, O LORD our God; for we
rest on thee.—2 CHRON. 14:11.

Help me to do thy holy will;
   Let duty bliss dispense;
Save from a disobedient heart,
   From sloth and negligence.

August

31. Though I have all faith, so that I could remove mountains, and have not charity, I am nothing.—1 Cor. 13:2.

> Oh, grant me, Lord, this one request,
>   And I'll be satisfied,—
> That love divine may rule my breast,
>   And all my actions guide.

September

1. That I might finish my course with joy.—Acts 20:24.

> With joy may we our course pursue,
>   And keep the crown of life in view,—
> That crown which in one hour repays
>   The labour of ten thousand days.

---

2. Behold, we come unto thee; for thou art the LORD our God.—JER. 3:22.

> Where but to the bleeding Saviour
>   Should we come for life and peace?
> Nothing but thy boundless favour
>   Can our burdened souls release.

September

3. Blessed is the man that trusteth in the
LORD.—JER. 17:7.

> I rest upon thy promise, Lord,
>   And trust thy love and power;
> Oh, make me more than conqueror now,
>   And in the final hour.

---

4. Lead me in thy truth, and teach me:
for thou art the God of my salvation.

—PSA. 25:5.

> Show me how vile I am by sin,
>   And wash me in thy cleansing blood;
> Oh, make me willing to be thine,
>   And be to me a cov'nant God.

September

5. Fight the good fight of faith, lay hold on eternal life.—1 Tim. 6:12.

> From strength to strength go on,
>   Wrestle, and fight, and pray;
> Tread all the powers of darkness down,
>   And win the well-fought day.

---

6. I meditate on all thy works; I muse on the work of thy hands.—Psa. 143:5.

> I love to think on miracles past,
>   And future good implore;
> And all my cares and sorrows cast
>   On him whom I adore.

September

7. Unto the upright there ariseth light in the darkness.—Psa. 112:4.

Lord, though my soul in darkness mourns,
    Thy word is all my stay;
Here would I rest till light returns—
    Thy presence makes my day.

———

8. Take ye heed, watch and pray: for ye know not when the time is.

—Mark 13:33.

The Saviour bids us watch and pray,
    For soon the hour will come
That calls us from the earth away
    To our eternal home.

September

9. What would ye that I should do for you?—MARK 10:36.

> Oh, grant me all a God can give,
>   And all that mortals can receive—
> Grace to believe in Jesus' blood,
>   Grace to enjoy and walk with God.

------

10. They looked unto him, and were lightened: and their faces were not ashamed.—PSA. 34:5.

> Look to the Lord, his word, his throne;
>   Look to his grace and not thine own:
> There wait and look, and look again,—
>   Thou shalt not wait nor look in vain.

September

11. He forgetteth not the cry of the humble.—Psa. 9:12.

The humble have the clearest light,
Who make the Lord their only stay:
Our knowledge, then, is sound and right,
When we repent, believe, obey.

———

12. O Lord of hosts, blessed is the man that trusteth in thee.—Psa. 84:12.

O, Lord of hosts, thou God of grace,
How blest, divinely blest, is he
Who trusts thy love, and seeks thy face,
And fixes all his hopes on thee.

September

13. O Lord, revive thy work in the midst of the years.—Hab. 3:2.

Oh, let thy Spirit to my heart
  Once more his quick'ning aid impart:
My mind from every fear release,
  And soothe my troubled thoughts to peace.

---

14. Amend your ways and your doings, and obey the voice of the Lord your God.—Jer. 26:13.

Blest are those servants who obey,
  Whatever ills betide;
Tho' snares and deaths before them lay,
  Faithful they still abide.

September

15. And rejoice in hope of the glory of God.—ROM. 5:2.

Soon shall close thy earthly mission,
  Soon shall pass thy pilgrim days;
Hope shall change to glad fruition,
  Faith to sight, and prayer to praise.

---

16. The earth shall be full of the knowledge of the LORD, as the waters cover the sea.—ISA. 11:9.

O let the kingdoms of the world
  Become the kingdoms of the Lord!
Let saints and angels praise thy name,
  Be thou thro' heaven and earth adored.

September

17. Ask, and it shall be given you; seek, and ye shall find; knock, and it shall be opened unto you.—MATT. 7:7.

Sweet precept and sweet promise Lord!
   I'll ask, encouraged by thy word:
Now shall my wants be all supplied,
   For Christ has promised, Christ has died!

18. The Lord preserveth the simple: I was brought low, and he helped me.

—PSA. 116:6.

Oh! may I ne'er forget
   The mercy of my God;
Nor ever want a tongue to spread
   His loudest praise abroad.

September

19. What shall I do, Lord?—Acts 22:10.

To him who on the fatal tree
   Poured out his blood, his life for me,
In grateful strains my voice I'll raise,
   And in his service spend my days.

---

20. Being now justified by his blood, we shall be saved from wrath through him.—Rom. 5:9.

For this he came and dwelt on earth,
   For this his life was given,
For this he fought and vanquished Death,
   For this he pleads in heaven.

September

21. The world passeth away, and the lust thereof.—1 JOHN 2:17.

> Lord, from this world call off my love,
>   Set my affections right;
> Bid me aspire to joys above,
>   And walk no more by sight.

---

22. If any man hear my voice, and open the door, I will come in to him, and will sup with him, and he with me.

—REV. 3:20.

> Enter my heart, Redeemer blest;
>   Enter, thou ever-honoured Guest;
> Enter, and make my heart thine own,
>   Thy house, thy temple, and thy throne.

23. Christ also loved the church, and gave himself for it.—EPH. 5:25.

> Sure there was never love so free,
>   Dear Saviour, so divine!
> Well mayest thou claim that heart of me,
>   Which owes so much to thine.

---

24. Whatsoever ye shall ask in my name, that will I do, that the Father may be glorified in the Son.—JOHN 14:13.

> Then let his name for ever be
>   To us supremely dear;
> Our only all-prevailing plea,
>   For all our hope is there.

September

25. We look not at the things which are seen, but at the things which are not seen.—2 COR. 4:18.

> I love by faith to take a view
>   Of brighter scenes in heaven;
> The prospect doth my faith renew,
>   While here by tempests driven.

———

26. Thou hast considered my trouble; thou hast known my soul in adversities.

—PSA. 31:7.

> Though Heaven afflicts, I'll not repine,
>   Each heartfelt comfort still is mine;
> Comforts that shall o'er death prevail,
>   And journey with me through the vale.

27. Jesus wept. Then said the Jews, Behold how he loved him!—JOHN 11:35, 36.

> Still his compassions are the same,
>   He knows the frailty of our frame;
> Our heaviest burdens he sustains,
>   Shares in our sorrows and our pains.

---

28. One is your Master, even Christ; and all ye are brethren.—MATT. 23:8.

> Jesus my Master now I call,
>   And consecrate to him my all:
> Lord, let me live and die to thee,
>   Be thine through all eternity.

September

29. My son, give me thine heart.
—PROV. 23:26.

> Yes, thou shalt surely have my heart,
>   My soul, my strength, my all;
> With life itself I'll freely part,
>   My Jesus, at thy call.

---

30. He shall stand at the right hand of the poor, to save him from those that condemn his soul.—PSA. 109:31.

> In prosperity be near,
>   To preserve me in thy fear;
> In affliction let thy smile
>   All the woes of life beguile.

October

1. One is your Father, which is in heaven.
—MATT. 23:9.

Art thou my Father? I'll depend
   Upon the care of such a friend;
And only wish to do and be
   Whatever seemeth good to thee.

———————

2. The God of peace shall bruise Satan
under your feet shortly.—ROM. 16:20.

Let Satan do his worst,
   And he his worst will do;
But I have made the Lord my trust,
   And he will bring me through.

October

3. Who then is willing to consecrate his
service this day unto the Lord?

—1 Chron. 29:5.

Fain would I now surrender make
 Of my whole self to thee;
Jesus, the humble offering take,
 Unworthy though it be.

———————

4. I will bless the Lord, who hath given
me counsel.—Psa. 16:7.

His counsels and upholding care
 My safety and my comfort are;
And he shall guide me all my days,
 Till glory crown the work of grace.

October

5. Thou art my hope, O Lord God: thou art my trust from my youth.—Psa. 71:5.

> In early years thou was my guide,
>   And of my youth the friend;
> And as my days began with thee,
>   With thee my days shall end.

---

6. But it is good for me to draw near to God.—Psa. 73:28.

> O teach me, Lord, to wait thy will,
>   To be content with all thou dost;
> For me thy grace sufficient still,
>   With most supplied when needing most.

October

7. He that taketh not his cross, and fol-
loweth after me, is not worthy of me.

—MATT. 10:38.

To them the cross with all its shame,
With all its grace is given;
Their name—an everlasting name;
Their joy—the joy of heaven.

---

8. Hope thou in God: for I shall yet
praise him.—PSA. 42:11.

Why, when storms around you gather,
Should your trembling spirits sink?
Look to God, your heavenly Father,
And of his sweet promise think.

October

9. Deliver me, O Lord, from mine enemies: I flee unto thee to hide me.

—Psa. 143:9.

Let me in thy name confide,
　Let me in thy bosom hide;
There in safety would I stay
　Till the storm has passed away.

---

10. I have chosen thee in the furnace of affliction.—Isa. 48:10.

In the furnace God is nigh,
　Feels our troubles, hears our cry;
Brings us out, and by it proves
　That he chastens whom he loves.

October

11. I said, I shall not see the Lord, even
the Lord, in the land of the living.

—Isa. 38:11.

Fancy will be often painting
  Scenes in dark and fearful shade;
Yet why should thy soul be fainting,
  Of prospective woes afraid?

———————

12. Walk worthy of the vocation where-
with ye are called.—Eph. 4:1.

Where is that holy walk that suits
  The name and character we bear?
And where are seen those heavenly fruits
  That show we're not what once we were?

October

13. That ye may be counted worthy of the kingdom of God, for which ye also suffer.—2 Thess. 1:5.

> They suffer with their Lord below,
>   They reign with him above;
> Their profit and their joy to know
>   The mystery of his love.

---

14. Say ye to the righteous that it shall be well with him.—Isa. 3:10.

> 'Tis well when on the mount
>   They feast on Jesus' love;
> And 'tis as well, in God's account,
>   When they the furnace prove.

October

15. I would seek unto God, and unto God would I commit my cause.

—JOB 5:8.

Resign, and all the load of life,
    That moment you remove;
Its heavy tax, ten thousand cares,
    Devolve on One above.

---

16. When he hath tried me, I shall come forth as gold.—JOB 23:10.

Saints indeed are sorely tried,
    Troubles rise on every side;
Nor are they exempt within—
    Nothing tries like inward sin.

October

17. All power is given unto me in heaven and in earth.—MATT. 28:18.

All power to Christ is given;
  He ever reigns the same;
Salvation, happiness, and heaven,
  Are all in Jesus' name.

---

18. The Lord preserveth all them that love him.—PSA. 145:20.

Saints are always in his keeping,
  And he always keeps them well;
Rising, resting, waking, sleeping,
  He preserves from death and hell.

October

19. Shall he that contendeth with the Almighty instruct him?—Job 40:2.

> I would not contend with thy will,
>   Whatever that will may decree;
> But oh, may each trial I feel
>   Unite me more firmly to thee.

---

20. Thou in faithfulness hast afflicted me.—Psa. 119:75.

> 'Tis sweet, though trials may not cease,
>   Though pains afflict, though fears appal,
> To feel my comforts still increase,
>   And say, 'My Father sends them all.'

October

21. Will the Lord cast off for ever? and will he be favourable no more?

—Psa. 77:7.

> Cease that dark anticipation,
> Still let love and faith abound;
> For the day of tribulation
> Strength sufficient will be found.

---

22. That your faith and hope might be in God.—1 Pet. 1:21.

> Let tempests rage, and billows rise,
> And mortal firmness shrink;
> Our anchor fastens in the skies,
> Our bark no storm can sink.

October

23. And he, bearing his cross, went forth into a place called Golgotha.

—JOHN 19:17.

> The cross he bore is life and health,
>   Though shame and death to him;
> His people's hope, his peoples' wealth,
>   Their everlasting theme.

---

24. Brethren, the time is short.

—1 COR. 7:29.

> The time is short; oh, who can tell
>   How short his time below may be?
> To-day on earth, his soul may dwell,
>   To-morrow in eternity.

October

25. He giveth power to the faint; and to them that have no might he increaseth strength.—Isa. 40:29.

> He gives the conquest to the weak,
>   Supports the sinking heart;
> And courage in the evil hour,
>   His heavenly aids impart.

---

26. My beloved is mine, and I am his.
                    —Song of Sol. 2:16.

> If Christ is mine, then all is mine,
>   And more than angels know;
> Both present things, and things to come,
>   And grace and glory too.

October

27. Teach us to number our days, that we may apply our hearts unto wisdom.

—PSA. 90:12.

Almighty Maker of my frame,
  Teach me the measure of my days;
Teach me to learn how frail I am,
  And spend the remnant to thy praise.

---

28. I will give them an heart to know me.—JER. 24:7.

Give me thyself: from every boast,
  From every wish set free;
Let all I am in thee be lost,
  But give thyself to me.

October

29. Zion said, The Lord hath forsaken
me, and my Lord hath forgotten me.

—Isa. 49:14.

The tender parent may forget,
The infant she hath nursed with care;
But God has ne'er forgotten yet
One soul that sought his face by prayer.

---

30. Be not faithless, but believing.

—John 20:27.

From faithlessness our sorrows flow;
Short-sighted mortals, weak and blind,
Bend down their eyes to earth and woe,
And doubt if Providence is kind.

October

31. I am God, even thy God.—Psa. 50:7.

I am thy God,—well, think of this
    When all things seem to go amiss;
This turns the darkest night to day,
    And saves the heart from sad dismay.

November

1. Behold, here am I, let him do to me as seemeth good unto him.—2 SAM. 15:26.

Fill my heart with deep contrition,
   Take away the heart of stone;
And may I, with true submission,
   Meekly say, 'Thy will be done!'

———

2. Rejoice evermore. Pray without ceasing.—1 THESS. 5:16, 17.

In every joy that crowns my days,
   In every pain I bear;
My heart shall find delight in praise,
   Or seek relief in prayer.

November

3. As he which hath called you is holy, so be ye holy in all manner of conversation.—1 PET. 1:15.

> Pure may I be, averse to sin,
>   Just, holy, merciful, and true;
> And let thine image, formed within,
>   Shine out in all I speak and do.

---

4. Behold the fear of the Lord, that is wisdom.—JOB 28:28.

> Who wisdom find are truly blessed,
>   The tree of life is then possessed;
> Of all that's valued this is best—
>   'Tis present and eternal rest.

November

5. God is our refuge and strength, a very present help in trouble.—Psa. 46:1.

> What troubles can their hearts o'erwhelm
>   Who view a Saviour near;
> Whose Father sits and guides the helm,
>   Whose voice forbids their fear?

―――――

6. To wait for his Son from heaven.
—1 Thess. 1:10.

> We wait the coming of our Lord,
>   Nor do we wait that day in vain;
> We cannot doubt his faithful word,
>   That tells us he will come again.

November

7. I will restore comforts unto him, and to his mourners.—ISA. 57:18.

> Drooping mourner canst thou languish,
>   Near the great Consoler's feet?
> He can give thee joy for anguish;
>   Seek him at the mercy-seat.

---

8. Their righteousness is of me, saith the LORD.—ISA. 54:17.

> Fear not, believer, thou art mine;
>   Rejoice and triumph in my name:
> My strength and righteousness are thine;
>   Thou never shalt be put to shame.

November

9. Rejoicing in hope; patient in tribulation; continuing instant in prayer.

—Rom. 12:12.

If Providence our comforts abound,
    And dark distresses lower,
Hope prints its rainbow on the cloud,
    And grace shines through the shower.

---

10. A friend of publicans and sinners.

—Matt. 11:19.

We need not be ashamed to own
    That he on whom our hopes depend,
Though now he fills the highest throne,
    Was styled on earth *the sinners' friend.*

11. Do justly, love mercy, and walk humbly with thy God.—MIC. 6:8.

In vain we talk of Jesus' blood,
   And boast his name in vain,
If we can slight the laws of God,
   And prove unjust to men.

---

12. He is the head of the body, the church.—COL. 1:18.

All our immortal hopes are laid
   In thee our Surety and our Head!
Thy cross, thy cradle, and thy throne,
   Are big with glories yet unknown.

13. As for me, I will call upon God; and the LORD shall save me.—PSA. 55:16.

> When disciplined by long distress,
>   And led through paths of fear and woe,
> Say, dost thou love thy children less?
>   No, ever-gracious Father—no.

---

14. The Amen, the faithful and true witness.—REV. 3:14.

> Jesus, the Faithful Witness now,
>   Speak by thy Spirit to my heart;
> Before thy throne my soul I bow,
>   Oh, bid my doubts and fears depart!

15. Greater love hath no man than this, that a man lay down his life for his friends.—JOHN 15:13.

Jesus hath died that I might live,
    Might live to God alone;
In him eternal life receive,
    And be in spirit one.

––––––––

16. The God of my mercy shall prevent me.—PSA. 59:10.

Let mercy, Lord, prevent me still,
    And guard my soul from every ill;
Let mercy compass me around,
    And guide me safe to Canaan's ground.

November

17. God according to his promise raised unto Israel a Saviour, Jesus.

—Acts 13:23.

A Saviour doubles all my joys,
  And sweetens all my pains;
His strength in my defence employs,
  Consoles me and sustains.

———

18. Where I am, there shall also my servant be.—John 12:26.

Where Jesus is, 'tis heaven to be,
  'Tis heaven the Saviour's face to see;
We know, though all the world revile,
  Celestial joy is in his smile.

November

19. Because of his strength will I wait upon thee: for God is my defence.

—PSA. 59:9.

Then let my trembling soul be still,
 Thy purpose though I may not see;
I'll wait thy wise, thy holy will—
 All must be well since ruled by thee.

---

20. I have longed for thy salvation, O LORD.—PSA. 119:174.

View, dearest Lord, my longing heart,
 Which pants and sighs for thee!
And oh, thyself and heaven impart,
 For there I long to be.

November

21. And when the people complained, it displeased the LORD.—NUM. 11:1.

> Should Heaven with every wish comply,
>   Say, would the grant relieve the care?
> Perhaps the good for which we sigh,
>   Might change its name, and prove a snare.

———————

22. Thou didst hide thy face, and I was troubled.—PSA. 30:7.

> Still on his plighted love;
>   At all events rely;
> The very hidings of his face
>   Shall train thee up for joy.

November

23. Every one that loveth is born of God, and knoweth God.—1 JOHN 4:7.

This is the central point of bliss;
 'Tis all I ask, 'tis all I need:
My soul is rich possessed of this;
 Without it, I am poor indeed.

———

24. Unto us a child is born, unto us a son is given.—ISA. 9:6.

My God, my Creator the heavens did bow
 To ransom offenders, and stooped very
 low;
The body prepared by his Father assumes,
 And on the kind errand most joyfully
 comes.

November

25. The Son of man is come to seek and to save that which was lost.

—LUKE 19:10.

This is a faithful, cheering word,
  That Jesus came to save the lost!
This truth with richest grace is stored,
  And to the vilest yields the most.

---

26. God is able to make all grace abound toward you.—2 COR. 9:8.

Plenteous grace with thee is found,
  Grace to pardon all my sin;
Let the healing streams abound,
  Make and keep me pure within.

November

27. The LORD of hosts is with us; the God of Jacob is our refuge.—PSA. 46:7.

God is our joy and portion still,
    When earthly good retires;
And shall our hearts sustain and fill,
    When earth itself expires.

---

28. Men ought always to pray, and not to faint.—LUKE 18:1.

Then let us pray, and never faint;
    The prayer of faith can all things do:
Employing this, the feeblest saint
    Can meet and vanquish every foe.

29. All things are of God, who hath reconciled us to himself by Jesus Christ.

—2 Cor. 5:18.

In each event of life, how clear
   Thy ruling hand I see;
Each blessing to my soul more dear,
   Because conferred by thee.

---

30. The desire of the righteous shall be granted.—Prov. 10:24.

To thee, O Lord, I look alone;
   To thee, to whom all hearts are known;
To walk with thee my soul aspires;
   Oh, satisfy my soul's desires.

December

1. To give you an inheritance among all them which are sanctified.—ACTS 20:32.

Our souls aspire to nobler things,
    Beyond the world our portion lies;
Our Father is the King of kings,
    And gives us everlasting joys.

————

2. God hath given us everlasting consolation and good hope through grace.

—2 THESS. 2:16.

Grace supports us, grace unbounded;
    Hope would perish but for this:
All our hope on grace is founded;
    O that sound, how sweet it is!

December

3. Ask for the old paths, where is the good way, and walk therein, and ye shall find rest for your souls.—JER. 6:16.

Were once our vain desires subdued,
    The will resigned, the heart at rest,
In every scene we should conclude
    The will of Heaven is right and best.

———

4. Thy God whom thou servest continually, he will deliver thee.—DAN. 6:16.

Through waves, and clouds, and storms,
    He gently clears thy way;
Wait but his time—thy darkest night—
    Shall end in brightest day.

December

5. For when we were yet without strength, in due time Christ died for the ungodly.—Rom. 5:6.

> And couldst thou, my Saviour, die,
> To rescue me from endless woe?
> Enough! there's none more blest than I,
> Since thou couldst love a sinner so.

---

6. The God of all grace hath called us unto his eternal glory by Christ Jesus.

—1 Pet. 5:10.

> Grace! 'tis a sweet, a charming theme;
> My thoughts rejoice at Jesus' name:
> Ye angels, dwell upon the sound;
> Ye heavens, reflect it to the ground.

December

7. All things were made by him; and without him was not any thing made that was made.—JOHN 1:3.

By his own power were all things made;
   By him supported all things stand;
He is the whole creation's Head,
   And angels fly at his command.

---

8. His mercy is on them that fear him from generation to generation.

—LUKE 1:50.

To those that fear and trust the Lord,
   His mercy stands for ever sure;
From age to age his promise lives,
   And the performance is secure.

December

9. Believe on the Lord Jesus Christ, and thou shalt be saved.—Acts 16:31.

With melting heart to him apply;
    Believe, and you shall never die:
Your souls, your all, to Jesus give;
    For he has bled that you might live.

---

10. He is despised and rejected of men; a man of sorrows, and acquainted with grief.—Isa. 53:3.

Rejected and despised of men,
    Behold a man of woe!
Grief was his close companion still,
    Through all his life below.

December

11. Say to them that are of a fearful heart, Be strong, fear not.—ISA. 35:4.

Shall I distrust my Saviour's love,
　Or doubt his promised grace?
Sooner shall rocks and hills remove
　Than his compassions cease.

---

12. Who hath blessed us with all spiritual blessings in heavenly places in Christ.
—EPH. 1:3.

Father, I wait thy daily will;
　Thou shalt divide my portion still;
Grant me on earth what seems thee best,
　Till death and heaven reveal the rest.

December

13. Who for the joy that was set before him endured the cross, despising the shame.—HEB. 12:2.

> Oh, the sweet wonders of that cross,
>   Where God the Saviour loved and died!
> Her noblest life my spirit draws
>   From his dear wounds and bleeding side.

---

14. Unto them that look for him shall he appear the second time without sin unto salvation.—HEB. 9:28.

> Now seated on his glorious throne,
>   He soon will come to claim his own;
> Soon shall they join his countless train,
>   Nor sin nor death afflict again.

December

15. Seek not ye what ye shall eat, or what ye shall drink, neither be ye of doubtful mind.—LUKE 12:29.

Oh, save me from the dreadful snare
  Of discontent and worldly care!
Lest I through unbelief depart
  From thee with an unthankful heart.

---

16. Little children, your sins are forgiven you for his name's sake.—1 JOHN 2:12.

My soul, forget not what is due
  To him whose suffering pardon brings;
Nor cease to keep the cross in view—
  The cross will teach thee wondrous things.

December

17. Put ye on the Lord Jesus Christ, and make not provision for the flesh.

—ROM. 13:14.

Make not provision for the flesh,
  But mortify its powers;
Put on the Saviour with his grace,
  And victory shall be yours.

---

18. Whatsoever thy hand findeth to do, do it with thy might.—ECCLES. 9:10.

Whate'er our hands shall find to do,
  Today may we with zeal pursue;
Seize fleeting moments as they fly,
  And *live* as we would *wish* to *die*.

December

19. Blessed are they that hear the word of God, and keep it.—LUKE 11:28.

To read thy word my heart incline;
    To understand it, light impart;
O Saviour, make me wholly thine!
    Take full possession of my heart.

———

20. Why art thou cast down, O my soul? and why art thou disquieted within me?
—PSA. 43:5.

Why, O my soul, why thus depressed,
    And whence this anxious fear?
Let former favours fix thy trust,
    And check the rising tear.

December

21. We trust in the living God, who is the Saviour of all men, specially of those that believe.—1 TIM. 4:10.

> Faith finds each promise sure;
>   Hope looks within the veil;
> Love bears the discipline divine,
>   And cleaves to Jesus still.

---

22. Truly my soul waiteth upon God: from him cometh my salvation.

—PSA. 62:1.

> I wait the visits of thy grace,
>   My Saviour and my God;
> O come and show thy smiling face,
>   And wash me in thy blood.

December

23. Blessed are they that mourn: for they shall be comforted.—MATT. 5:4.

They're blessed on earth, for 'tis by grace
    They see and know their mournful case;
Blessed mourners! they shall shortly rise
    To endless comfort in the skies.

---

24. Behold, my witness is in heaven, and my record is on high.—JOB 16:19.

My soul, arise! shake off thy fears,
    And wipe thy sorrows dry;
Jesus in heaven thy witness bears,
    Thy record is on high.

December

25. Looking for the mercy of our Lord
Jesus Christ unto eternal life.—Jude 21.

Thy mercy, O my gracious Lord,
　Can all my guilt and fears remove;
In life and death can help afford
　And fit me for the realms above.

———

26. The Lamb slain from the foundation
of the world.—Rev. 13:8.

The Lord in the day of his anger did lay,
　Our sins on the Lamb, and he bore them
　　away;
He died to atone for sins not his own;
　The Father hath punish'd for us his dear
　　Son.

December

27. Beware lest thou forget the LORD.
                              —DEUT. 6:12.

My sinful nature proves indeed
  That I this caution daily need:
Oh, may it in my heart be stored—
  Beware, lest thou forget the Lord.

---

28. Jesus Christ is the faithful witness,
and the first begotten of the dead.

                              —REV. 1:5.

He promis'd a crown when he left us a cross,
  A kingdom we gain, the reward of our loss:
To glory he leads, and to him let us cleave:
  The faithful true Witness will never deceive.

December

29. I will give unto him that is athirst of the fountain of the water of life freely.

—Rev. 21:6.

Come, then, with all your wants and wounds
  Your every burden bring;
Here love, eternal love, abounds,
  A deep celestial spring.

---

30. That ye may stand perfect and complete in all the will of God.—Col. 4:12.

Grace will complete what grace begins,
  To save from sorrows and from sins:
The work that Wisdom undertakes
  Eternal Mercy ne'er forsakes.

December

31. Him that overcometh will I make a pillar in the temple of my God, and he shall go no more out.—Rev. 3:12.

> A few successful struggles yet,
>   Then not a conflict more!
> Satan and sin shall ne'er assault
>   On the celestial shore.

1 ✓

2

The Banner of Truth Trust originated in 1957 in London. The founders believed that much of the best literature of historic Christianity had been allowed to fall into oblivion and that, under God, its recovery could well lead not only to a strengthening of the church, but to true revival.

Interdenominational in vision, this publishing work is now international, and our lists include a number of contemporary authors, together with classics from the past. The translation of these books into many languages is encouraged.

A monthly magazine, *The Banner of Truth*, is also published, and further information about this, and all our other publications, may be found on our website, banneroftruth.org, or by contacting the offices below:

Head Office:
3 Murrayfield Road
Edinburgh, EH12 6EL
United Kingdom

Email:
info@banneroftruth.co.uk

North America Office:
610 Alexander Spring Road
Carlisle, PA 17015
United States of America

Email:
info@banneroftruth.org